Awesome Not Autism!

Written & Illustrated By

Sharon L. Stevens

Copyright © 2022

All Rights Reserved

Dedication

I dedicate this book to Ray'Jabeon, who God used to inspire me to write this book. I'm so blessed to have you in my life as a great helper in the ministry and as a wonderful grandson.

Acknowledgments

I want to acknowledge my awesome husband and close friend, Charles, who has had my back from day one. You are heaven-sent. I'm glad you are in my life.

My precious children, Emmanuel, Tabiyus, Shaterri - I am so glad to be your mother. You three are dear to my heart.

My grandchildren, Ray'Jabeon, My'Angel, Elias, and Brooke'Lynn - Words can't explain the special place that I have for you in my heart.

My mother, Margie - I love you, and I appreciate you for all you have done for me.

All my siblings and Cynthia, a special sister - I truly love you all for making my life complete.

My nieces and nephews, church family - Thank you so much for being part of my life. It's such a blessing, much love.

About the Author

Apostle Sharon Stevens is a retiree from the Department of Social Services. She is a wife, mother of three, and grandmother of four. She is the owner of Christian Way Academy and Sharon's Miracle Hands Company, and the founder of Moving By The Spirit of God Ministries. INC. 1 and 2. Most importantly, she is a pastor who loves to travel, preach and teach the word of God—letting people know that there's hope in God. With him, you can make it!

Apostle Sharon resides in the North Carolina area with her family.

Oh wow! What a restless night I had, tossing and turning in my bed, wondering how the day would be in my new classroom, with people I don't even know.

I was diagnosed with Autism Spectrum Disorder (ASD) and, therefore, sometimes have difficulty interacting and responding to the world around me.

I continued to cry while words came delayed, delayed in and out of my mind as I tried to sleep. It seemed that the thoughts would never end.

Before I knew it, the sun was rising, and my mother was at the door, shouting, "Get up! Get up! Rise and shine. We don't want to be late on your big, big day."

I replied to my mother, "Okay," in a sad trembling voice. She immediately noticed my lack of enthusiasm. "My dear, what's wrong? You're not excited about meeting new friends today, are you? The silence was between us for a moment too long. I couldn't speak and express how I was feeling.

As I was getting ready for school, in my mind, all I could think of at that time was: Get yourself ready for lots of challenges. Finally, I gathered up the courage to respond to my mother. "Hello Mom, could we talk, please? She immediately answered, "Sure, I'm all ears."

As I sat down at the table for breakfast, my body language was all over the place, and I was at a loss for words. Again I couldn't speak, not knowing how to put my words together. I thought: Oh, this is just great! Feeling so confused, I took a deep breath to relax while thinking how and what I was going to say to my mother.

I thought: This is not good at all! I can't even communicate as I desire to with my own mom. How can I communicate with people who are strangers in my life?

Finally, my mother began to ask me to help me talk about what was troubling me. "My son, what's troubling you? You're not acting like yourself at all."

It just so happened the words started coming one word after the next at once. "Mother," I replied, "this is a huge challenge for me - communicating with new people on their level. Being autistic is disappointing."

Suddenly she grabbed me and wrapped her arms around me with encouraging words, saying, "Son, you are not autistic. You are awesome!" She then said, "I want you to always remember that God made you to be different."

Oh, boy, I was ready to meet my new teacher and classmates with confidence now, knowing that God created me to be who I was! Yes, yes, to be who I was. That meant I could do anything positive in life that I desired to do. Yes, yes! I am Awesome, not Autistic!

All the way to school, I had to remind myself over and over again. "Awesome, not Autistic." Finally, we arrived at school. As we were getting out of the car, my knees began to buckle because of being so afraid once more. Words started to repeat, coming out of my mouth one after another.

Before I knew it, we were entering my new classroom. My teacher was waiting at the door. She said with a smile, "Come on, welcome. My name is Ms. Angel Awesome. What is your name?" "My name is Faithdon Move.," I replied. Her last name stayed in my mind - 'Awesome'. Wow, I feel great, I thought to myself.

Ms. Awesome began to take me to my desk. While unpacking my things and placing them inside my desk, I began to speak to myself quietly. "My mother told me that I am Awesome, not Autistic. Secondly, my teacher's name is Angel Awesome. This is a wonderful day already!"

What a great sign that I could be awesome in everything I did, no matter where I was. Now the meet and greet was over. The classroom went quiet, and the work began. Ms. Awesome gave us our first assignment of the day, which was for us to stand up and tell the class about ourselves.

Oh no! I said to myself. How can this be? There's no way in this world I can do this. I can't stand up. I can't communicate very well. Interacting with others is a hard challenge for me. Why is this happening to me? Eye to eye isn't for me.

All of a sudden, out of nowhere, I remembered what my mother had told me. "You are awesome, not autistic." As soon as I had finished that thought, Ms. Awesome called my name. "Faithdon, would you please come in front of the class and tell us a little bit about yourself?" I stood up quickly and boldly with my head held up and walked down the aisle way.

Now standing in front of the class, I said, "Hello everyone, my name is Faithdon Move. It's nice to meet you all. I'm 8 years old. I like to sing, dance and ride my go-cart. My favorite colors are red, blue, and purple. My favorite food is hamburgers, fries and pizza. My favorite dessert is vanilla ice cream.

Yes, yes! My words didn't repeat and weren't delayed at all either. One word after the next kept flowing out of my mouth. They really understood what I was saying to them. Everyone in the class was listening to me attentively, some even smiled at me. The more I talked, the more confident I felt.

At the end of my conversation, I told them that I was diagnosed with ASD, and my teacher helped me explain clearly to the class what Autism Spectrum Disorder was.

I continued, "I'm not. I am awesome, not autistic. God created me to be awesome. I can do anything positive in life that I want to do. I can be anything in life that I want to be. I'm chosen to be different. I'm just special, that's all."

After my speech was over, my whole class stood up and began to clap their hands. They walked over to me and formed a group circle of hugs around me and said to me:

"You are Awesome, not Autistic!"

The End.

www.ingramcontent.com/pod-product-compliance
Lightning Source LLC
Chambersburg PA
CBHW060428010526
44118CB00017B/2407